MAP YOUR PLANET



# MOUNTAINS

ANNABEL SAVERY

Cavendish Square

Published in 2024 by Cavendish Square Publishing, LLC
2544 Clinton Street, Buffalo, NY 14224



Website: cavendishsq.com



Editor: Annabel Savery
Designer: Clare Nicholas
Series designer: Rocket Design (East Anglia) Ltd

The publisher would like to thank the following for permission to reproduce their pictures:
Getty: denizunlusu 3 (background) & 20(cl), dominikmichalek 4(t), Starcevic 5(t), PeterHermesFurian 6(b), Tinkivinki 7(t), shirophoto 8(cl) & 30, ToniFlap 8(br), CoreyFord 9(tl), Gooddenka 10–11, LightScribe 11(t), ePhotocorp 12(c), sihasakprachum 12(t), BenjaminSullivan 14(b), MariuszBlach 16(c), Photos.com 16(b), slobo 16–17(t), dpenn 17(t), Art Wager 17(bl), lucky-photographer 17(br), guenterguni 18 & 32, Star Tribune via Getty Images / Contributor 18(b), Eloi_Omella 19(t), denizunlusu 20(cl), travellinglight 20(br), nzgmw2017 21(tl), Goddard_Photography 21(tr), andersen_oystein 22(t), shoo_arts 22(br), Vadim_Nefedov 23, Art Wager 24(c), theartist312 24(br), wallix 25(t), mcbrugg 27(t), bonottomario 28(bl), happytrip 28(br), Maryna Patzen 29(br); NASA: 23(b); Shutterstock: Gorb Andrii cover & 1 (inset), pchais cover & 1 (main), Mubarak_Khan 2 & 26, Serban Bogdan 5(b), DG-Studio 6(t), Jakl Lubos 7(c), Joanna Rigby-Jones 7(b), VectorMine 10(t) & 14(t), Rainer Lesniewski 11(b), Oscity 15(t) & 31, VectorMine 19(b), Nicku 27(bl), Anton Shahrai 27(br).
Design elements from Shutterstock.
Map illustrations: Julian Baker: 9, 12–13, 17, 21, 24–25, 28–29.

Cataloging-in-Publication Data

Names: Savery, Annabel.
Title: Mountains / Annabel Savery.
Description: New York : Cavendish Square Publishing, 2024. | Series: Map your planet | Includes glossary and index.
Identifiers: ISBN 9781502668479 (pbk.) | ISBN 9781502668486 (library bound) | ISBN 9781502668493 (ebook)
Subjects: LCSH: Mountains--Juvenile literature.
Classification: LCC GB512.M563 2024 | DDC 551.43'2--dc23

CPSIA compliance information: Batch #CSCSQ24:
For further information contact Cavendish Square Publishing LLC at 1-877-980-4450.

Printed in the United States of America

# CONTENTS

What are mountains? ........ 4
Shifting Earth ........ 6
**Mapping the Ring of Fire** ........ 8
Fold mountains ........ 10
**Mapping the Himalayas** ........ 12
Faults and domes ........ 14
**Mapping the Sierra Nevada** ........ 16
On the plateau ........ 18
**Mapping New Zealand's volcanic plateau** ........ 20
Volcanic mountains ........ 22
**Mapping the Hawaiian Islands** ........ 24
People in the mountains ........ 26
**Mapping the Alps** ........ 28
Glossary ........ 30
Further information ........ 31
Index ........ 32

# WHAT ARE MOUNTAINS?

**Mountains are landforms that rise over 1,970 feet (600 m). They are usually drawn as rocky triangles with snowy tops, but they come in many shapes and sizes. Anything lower than 1,970 feet (600 m) is classified as a hill.**

Ready for adventure: climbers balance on a high ridge on Liskamm mountain in the Alps.

## RISING HIGH

Mountains are enormous landforms. They are so big that they influence the way the world forms around them. They affect weather patterns and water courses. This, in turn, affects where trees and plants grow, and where humans make settlements. Mountains can be home to many ecosystems, often with liveable terrain at the foothills that becomes more barren as the slopes rise.

## THE TALLEST PEAKS ON EACH CONTINENT

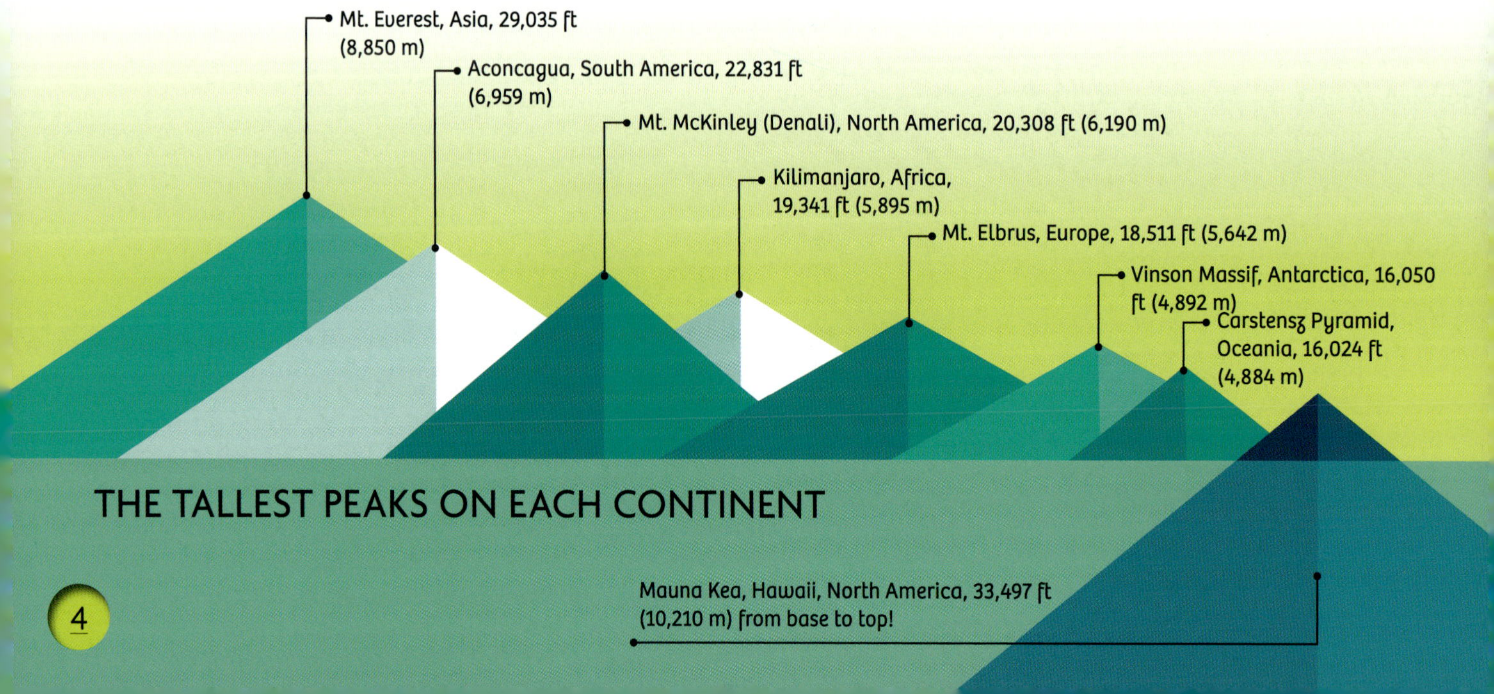

## MOUNTAIN RANGES

Mountains are rarely found as solitary peaks. They are usually part of a string or group of mountains, called a range. Mountain ranges can stretch for many miles. The longest mountain range is actually under the sea! The Mid-Atlantic Ridge extends from the Arctic Ocean to the southern tip of Africa. The longest range on the Earth's surface is the Andes, which runs along the west coast of South America.

The islands of the Azores are formed on the peaks of the Mid-Atlantic Ridge.

This map shows the height of ground levels in metres. The key tells you which colors are used for the heights above and below sea level (0 m, green).

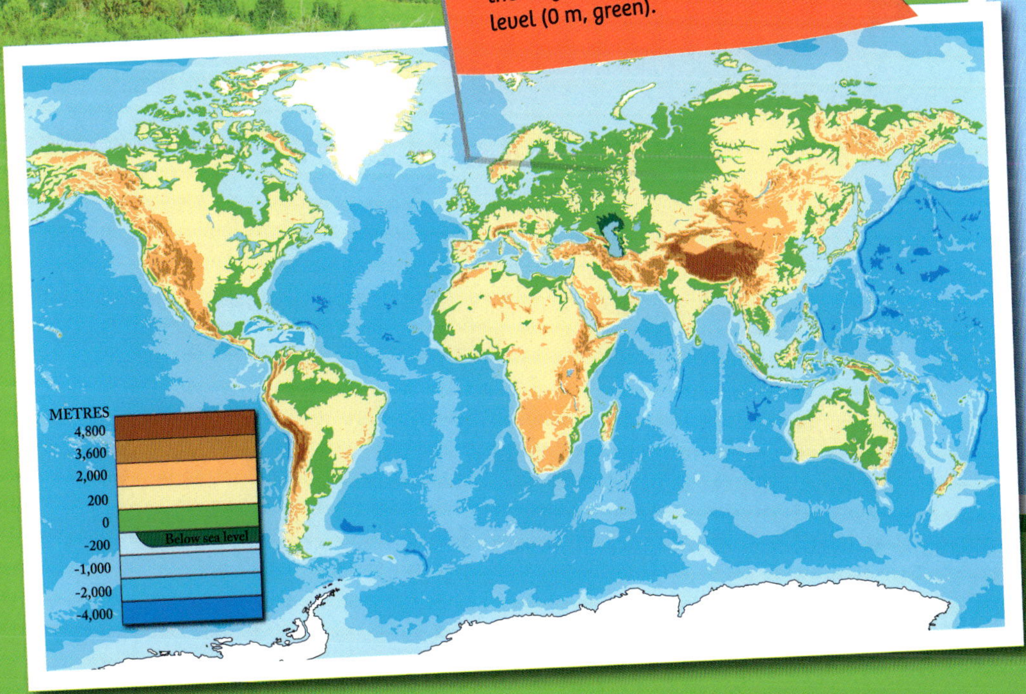


### MAP MASTERS

Maps are a great way to show information. Political maps show state and country borders, cities, and towns. Physical maps show land features, such as mountains, rivers, lakes, and forests. Maps can also give information about climate, population, road and rail networks, resources – almost anything!

# SHIFTING EARTH

**Mountains have formed through the constant shifting and changing of Earth's surface. The movement of Earth's crust comes from its structure. Let's take a look inside and see what's going on.**

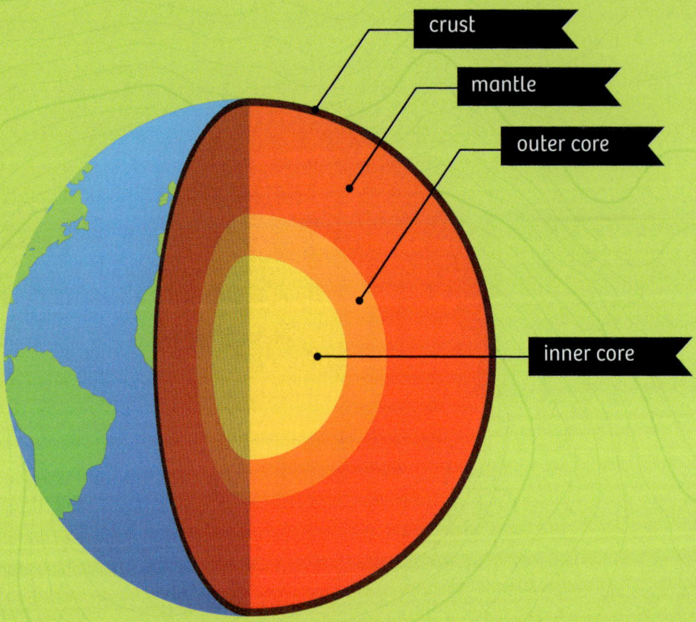


## ON THE MOVE

The ground we walk on is the Earth's crust. Below the crust is the mantle, made of hot, molten rock called magma. In the center is the core, made of iron and nickel. The outer core is liquid, but the inner core is solid. The crust is split into pieces called tectonic plates. As magma heats and cools below the crust, the mantle moves around. As the mantle moves, the plates move too.

## PLATE TECTONICS

Earth's surface is divided into seven major and eight minor plates. Some plates move towards each other, some pull apart, and others move horizontally against each other. As plate boundaries move against each other, mountains form as Earth's crust is pushed and pulled. Plate boundaries are also where most volcanoes and earthquakes happen.

Plates under the ocean are called oceanic plates. They can be 31-62 miles (50-100 km) thick. Plates that rise above the ocean are called continental plates and can be up to 124 miles (200 km) thick.

## MAP MASTERS

Around 299 million years ago, the Earth had one large landmass called Pangaea. Around 200 million years ago, the landmass began to break apart. Over time, the separate plates have moved and broken, forming the continent masses we have today.

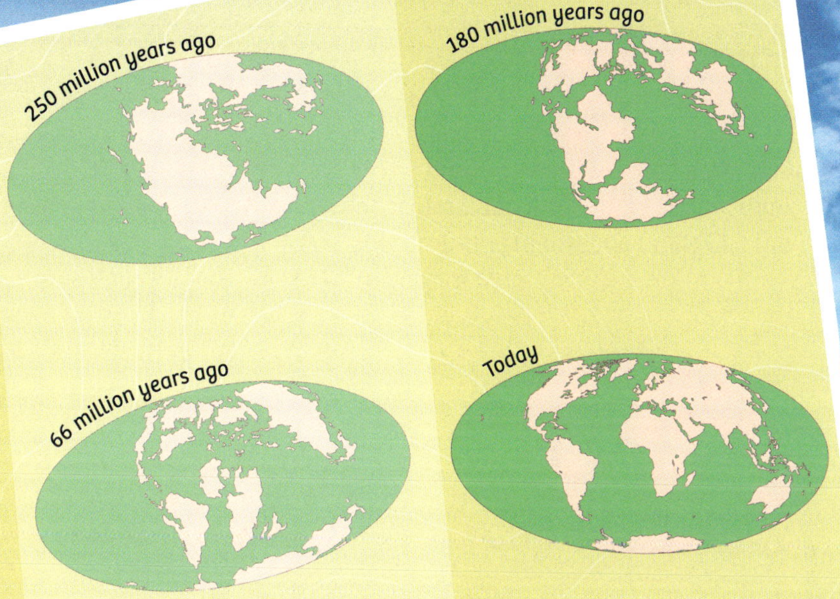

The Matterhorn in the Alps mountain range formed through a collision of the Eurasian and African Plates.

The Great Rift Valley in Africa has formed where the African and Arabian Plates pull apart.

# MAPPING THE RING OF FIRE

The movement of the Pacific Plate has led to many mountain formations. The boundary of the Pacific Plate has created so much volcanic activity that it has become known as the "Ring of Fire"!

## THE PACIFIC PLATE

**The Pacific Plate is one of the largest and is mainly oceanic crust. There are smaller plates around it, including the Philippine, Juan de Fuca, Cocos, and Nazca Plates (see pages 6–7). In most places, the oceanic Pacific Plate is slipping underneath the continental plates it meets. However, where the Pacific Plate meets the North American Plate, the two slide horizontally past each other, forming the San Andreas Fault. At the East Pacific Rise, the Pacific and Nazca Plates move apart.**

### 1 JAPAN AND MOUNT FUJI

Mount Fuji is Japan's highest mountain. It is formed from three volcanoes that are a result of the Pacific Plate being pushed under the Eurasian Plate. The highest volcano – Shin Fuji – continues to smolder and erupt.

### 2 THE ANDES

The Andes have formed through the collision of the Nazca Plate and the South American Plate. As the plates meet, the Nazca Plate is forced under the South American Plate, pushing the land upward. The land continues to move today, and Chile experienced devastating earthquakes in 1960 and 2010.

## CASCADE MOUNTAINS

The Cascade mountains extend up the west coast of the U.S., through the states of Oregon and Washington, to the Canadian border. Many peaks rise up over 9,840 feet (3,000 m) and are extinct volcanoes. Mount St. Helens is an active peak, which erupted in 1981 and between 2004 and 2008.

**FACT**

IT IS THOUGHT THAT MORE THAN 20,000 VOLCANIC MOUNTAINS HAVE FORMED ON THE OCEAN FLOORS AROUND THE WORLD.

# FOLD MOUNTAINS

**When continental plates collide, the Earth's crust can buckle and crease to form fold mountains.**

## PUSHING PLATES

Enormous pressure builds up at plate boundaries. When two landmasses push against each other, the rock at the plate edges is forced upward. Mountains formed in this way are called "fold" mountains. This change happens incredibly slowly, over millions of years. Fold mountains form steep, craggy peaks as chunks of rock are pushed upward.

In Russia's Ural Mountains, rocks have been forced upward, leaving steep ridges.

Over millions of years, ice and water have shaped the rocks of the Blue Ridge Mountains in the Appalachian Range to become the landscape we see today (see page 19).

## THE APPALACHIAN REVOLUTION

The Appalachian Mountains of North America are some of the oldest in the world. They formed 299 million years ago in an event called the Appalachian Revolution. At this time, great masses of underground rock were forced to buckle and fold, causing older rocks to be set on top of younger ones.

### MAP MASTERS

Maps use a small triangle to mark the summit of a mountain on a map. The height is marked in meters above sea level. But how do you know how steep the mountain is? Mapmakers use a system of contour lines. These lines mark places of the same height above sea level. Where the land climbs steeply, the lines are close together. Where it rises and falls gently, the lines are far apart.

# MAPPING THE HIMALAYAS

Phew! We've reached the highest mountain range on Earth. Here in the Himalayas there are 14 peaks that rise over 26,250 feet (8,000 m)!

## YOUNG MOUNTAINS

**The Himalayan range runs 1,550 miles (2,500 km) from east to west. The Himalayas are fold mountains formed by a collision between the Indian and Eurasian Plates just 33 million years ago. This makes them young when compared to other mountain ranges, and they are still moving!**

## 1 WEATHER WATCH

The height and position of the Himalayas means that they block cold winds coming from the north. They catch the warm monsoon rains that rise over India, causing rainfall on south-facing slopes. On the Indian side, there is lush rain forest fed by rivers that begin in the Himalayas. On the north side, a dry plateau (see page 18) stretches for many miles.

## 2 LIFE IN THE MOUNTAINS

The Sherpa people are a specific ethnic group, but it has also become a term for people who live in the region below Everest. Sherpas are excellent mountaineers and assist with climbing expeditions. They believe the mountains are homes to their gods, and trouble has arisen when foreign climbers burn trash or injure animals.

### HIGHEST PEAKS (IN METERS)

1. Everest, 8,850 m
2. K2, 8,612 m
3. Kanchenjunga, 8,586 m
4. Lhotse I, 8,516 m
5. Makalu I, 8,463 m
6. Cho Oyu, 8,201 m
7. Dhaulagiri, 8,167 m
8. Manaslu, 8,163 m
9. Nanga Parbat, 8,126 m
10. Annapurna, 8,091 m
11. Gasherbrum I, 8,068 m
12. Broad Peak, 8,047 m
13. Gasherbrum II, 8,035 m
14. Shisha Pangma, 8,012 m

Different ecosystems can be found here: from sparse alpine meadow on the higher slopes, through forest to tropical rain forest on the lower slopes.

### FACT

THE HIMALAYAS WERE FIRST MAPPED IN 1590!

## 3 EVEREST

Nine of the world's ten highest mountains are in the Himalayas. Everest is the tallest at 29,035 feet (8,850 m). The second highest is K2 at 28,255 feet (8,612 m) in the neighboring Karakoram Range – often considered part of the Himalayas.

# FAULTS AND DOMES

**These mountains form to create spectacular peaks with sheer edges and deep valleys.**

## FAULT-BLOCK FORMATIONS

Fault-block mountains form where there is a fault (crack) in the Earth's crust. When the tectonic plate shifts, the land around the fault is then forced downward or upward, creating mountains, valleys, and plateaus. Blocks are rarely pushed straight upward; they tilt and twist as they rise, creating a gentle slope on one side and a steep drop on the other.

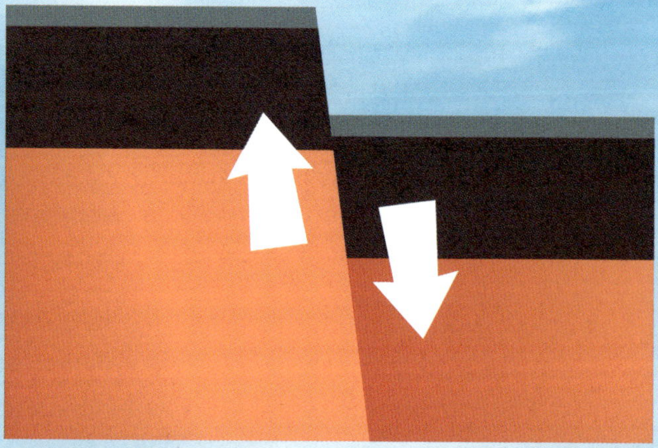

The Black Hills in South Dakota are thickly forested, leading to their dark appearance, and their tops are weathered into craggy formations. They formed through magma forcing the ground upward.

## DOME MOUNTAINS

There are many different types of rock making up the Earth's crust and some are harder than others. When magma moves around beneath the Earth's crust it is forced against the surface. At places where the rock is softer it can force the rock upward. If the magma is forced through the rock, you have a volcano. If the magma remains below the surface, a dome forms. The magma inside the dome cools and becomes hard rock. Over time, the softer rock on the surface can wear away, and a dome of harder rock is left.

Half Dome peak in Yosemite National Park, California, is an amazing example of a dome mountain.

### MAP MASTERS

Measuring mountains is a tricky business! Photogrammetry takes measurements from photographs by making them into 3D images. You can also use satellites, but this means taking receivers to the top of mountain summits, which isn't always practical. The simplest, and oldest, way is to measure the distance between two points on the ground, and then measure the angles to the mountain summit. Then the height can be calculated using the same equations you learn in school!

# MAPPING THE SIERRA NEVADA

**On the west coast of the United States is the dramatic Sierra Nevada. This high, tilted block of Earth's crust has been shaped through weather, time, and human activity.**

## EAST AND WEST

**A fault along the east of the range shows where a block of the Earth's crust lifted clear of the surface. The block tilted westward, creating a gentle slope along the western side and a steep drop along the east with a deep valley below it. Thousands of years ago, the whole area was covered with a glacial ice cap, causing massive erosion and the dramatic landforms we see today.**

### 1 LAKE TAHOE

To the northern end of the range is Lake Tahoe. This is the biggest alpine lake in the world, left from the time of the glaciers. Today, the clear waters are threatened with pollution.

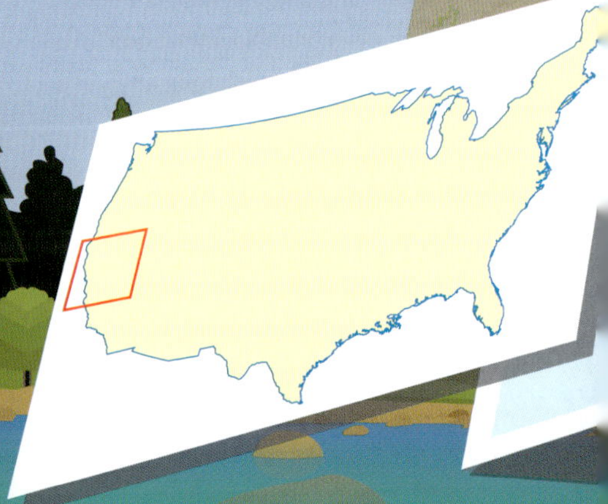

### 2 THE GOLD RUSH

This region was largely unaffected by the Native Americans who originally lived here. In 1848, gold was found in the American River, and this changed everything. Within two years, 50,000 mines had been established in the region, leading to massive industrial development and towns being established.

## 3 MOUNT WHITNEY

The highest peaks are in the south of the range. Mount Whitney is the highest peak at 14,495 feet (4,418 m). From here, the land drops away to the vast expanse of Death Valley - the lowest, driest, hottest place in North America.

## 4 YOSEMITE NATIONAL PARK

This national park has been a protected area since 1964. It is home to the world's tallest trees – the sequoias – estimated to be around 2,000 years old. Yosemite Valley was carved by ancient glaciers. The spectacular granite peaks include Half Dome and El Capitan.

# ON THE PLATEAU

**Mountain formation depends not only on what is happening beneath the crust, but also what the crust is made of, and what is happening on the surface.**

## PLATEAU MOUNTAINS

Plateaus are large areas of high, flat land. These might be created by uplift: when two tectonic plates collide and a section of land is raised upward. They can also be created by lava flow from a volcano (see page 22). As lava spreads around a volcano, it cools and hardens, adding to the landscape.

The Tibetan Plateau is a vast section of Earth's crust that has been raised upward. It stretches for 965,250 square miles ( 2,500,000 sq km).

### MAP MASTERS

Geology is the study of Earth and the substances it is made from. Geological maps show us what the ground is made up of. These are useful when it comes to planning. They can be used to show where groundwater is – in case there is a risk of contamination; to predict volcanic, earthquake, or landslide activity; to locate mineral resources; and to help with good management of land.

Geological maps of Minnesota show how groundwater is vulnerable to contamination.

## HOW MOUNTAINS CHANGE

Mountains are changing all the time. In many places, the tectonic forces that raised them are still active. Mountains also change with erosion. This is the process of weather, water, and ice wearing away parts of the mountain. When erosion happens over a long time, incredible shapes can be left behind.

Over thousands of years, water and weather have shaped the rock of the Grand Canyon in Arizona into spectacular formations.

## WEATHERING AND EROSION

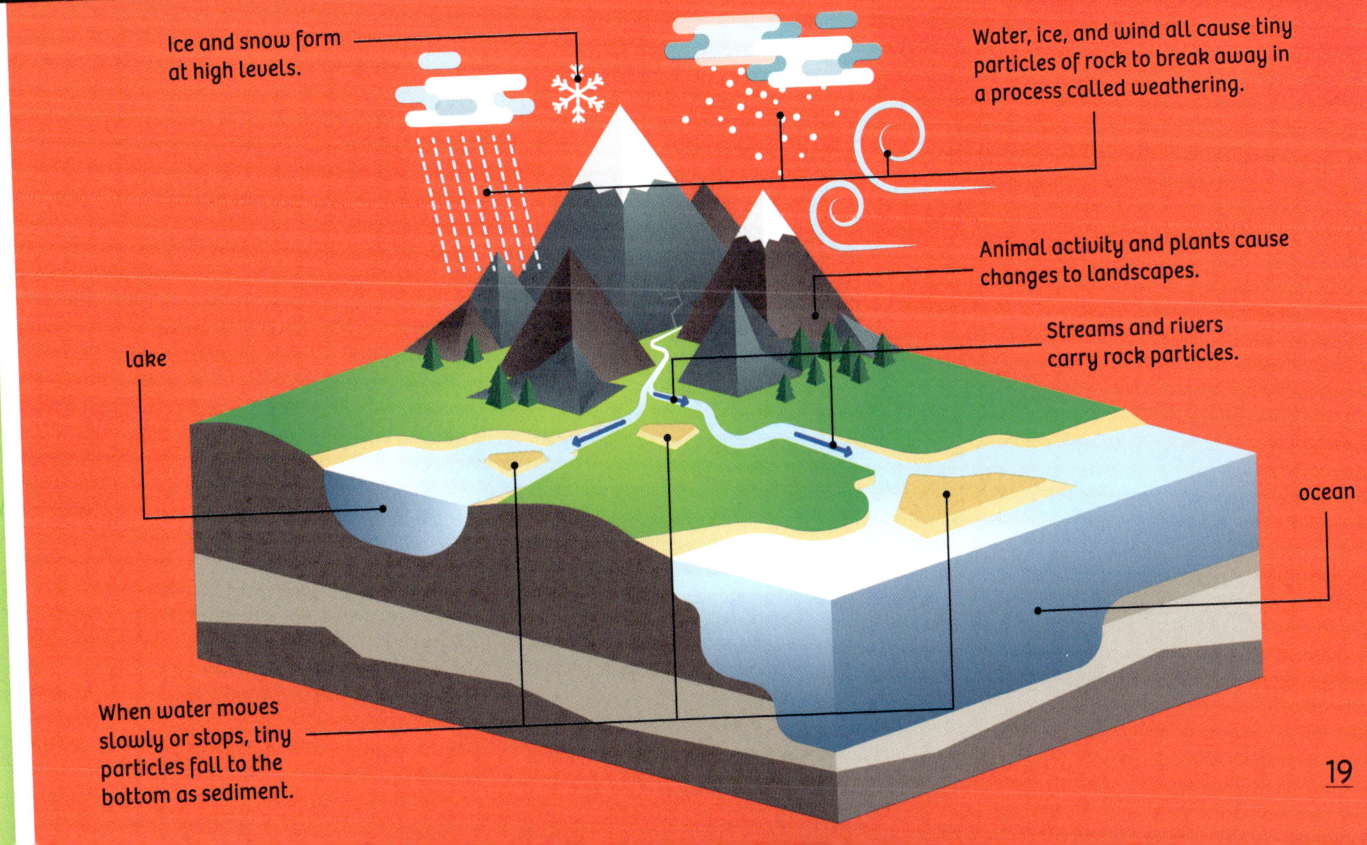

MAPPING
# NEW ZEALAND'S VOLCANIC PLATEAU

**New Zealand's North Island is home to a spectacular volcanic landscape.**

## VOLCANO ISLAND

**New Zealand's North Island sits on the Pacific Plate, while most of the South Island sits on the Indian–Australian Plate (see pages 6–7). The plates are being continuously pushed together, and the Pacific Plate is sinking beneath the Indian–Australian. This leads to volcanic activity on the North Island. As volcanoes have erupted, the lava, ash, and rock have formed a plateau.**

### 1 CRATER LAKES

The biggest eruptions have come from three volcanoes: Taupo, Okataina, and Rotorua. Their past eruptions have been so vast that the landscape and vegetation were buried beneath ash, rock, and lava. Today, the craters of these volcanoes have formed lakes, the biggest of which is Lake Taupo. The lake is fed by the Tongariro River, which runs down from Mount Ruapehu.

### 2 BUSY PEAKS

The three tallest peaks on the plateau are all active volcanoes. Their eruptions have been smaller but more recent. Mount Ngauruhoe is the most active volcano on the island; it last erupted between 1973 and 1975. Ruapehu is the tallest volcanic mountain on the island. Its eruption in 2007 created lahars – dangerous mudflows – in valleys nearby. Mount Tongariro is topped by active volcanic craters. The Te Maari crater was last active in 2012.

## 3 THE MAORI

The first people to settle on the islands were from Polynesia. When European settlers arrived, the original settlers took the name Maori, meaning "usual"or "ordinary", to distinguish themselves from the newcomers. The area of Tongariro National Park has become a protected site because of its importance to the Maori.

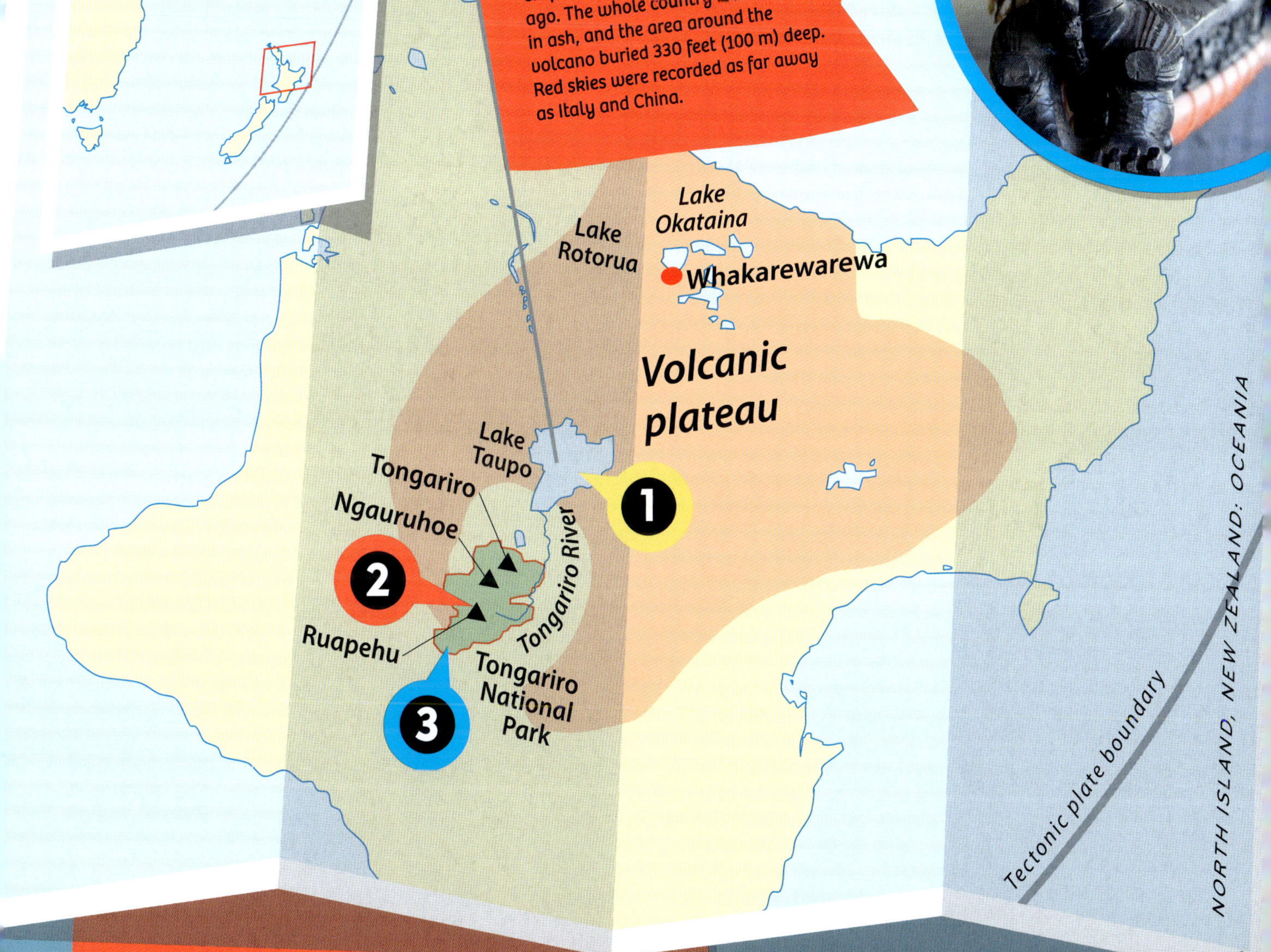


Taupo is a supervolcano. Its biggest eruption was around 1,800 years ago. The whole country was covered in ash, and the area around the volcano buried 330 feet (100 m) deep. Red skies were recorded as far away as Italy and China.

## FACT

THE GROUND HEATS UP TO SUCH A DEGREE AT WHAKAREWAREWA THAT WATER BOILS IN THE EARTH AND BURSTS OUT AS HOT SPRINGS AND GEYSERS!

# VOLCANIC MOUNTAINS

**Volcanic mountains can tower above the landscape as great cone shapes. Active volcanoes can erupt with little warning, sending hot ash, smoke, and molten rock high into the air!**

Anak Krakatau (Child of Krakatoa) in Indonesia rose above sea level as an active volcano between 1927 and 1930. The volcano is still active today and is now 984 feet (300 m) above sea level.

## HOTSPOTS

Volcanoes form at plate boundaries and over hotspots. Hotspots are areas in the middle of plates where heat and pressure melt the rock of the crust and force the magma through. As tectonic plates move and different areas are moved over the hotspot, the old volcanoes become dormant and new volcanoes form. This creates volcanic chains.

## WHAT ARE VOLCANOES?

Volcanoes form when hot magma from beneath the Earth's crust forces its way to the surface. Magma emerging from a volcano is called lava. As lava cools, it forms slopes on either side of the volcano's cone. As the lava continues to pour out, the slopes on either side are built up and the mountain forms.

## DANGER ZONE

People can live on the slopes of a volcano, even if it is active. There are benefits that can outweigh the danger. Volcanoes often attract visitors and this tourism brings employment for local people. In places where volcanic ash has fallen in the past, the land can be fertile and good for growing crops. Rich mineral deposits can also be found around volcanoes.

Fertile farmland sits below volcanoes in Rwanda's Volcanoes National Park.

### MAP MASTERS

There are thought to be around 1,500 active volcanoes around the world. It is hard to monitor all of them, but new satellite systems can help. As a volcano gets ready to erupt, the magma rises below the surface, causing small changes to the area around the crater. This can't be seen by the human eye, but it can be seen from space.

This is a satellite image of Shiveluch, one of the largest and most active volcanoes on Russia's Kamchatka Peninsula.

# MAPPING THE HAWAIIAN ISLANDS

**Welcome to the islands of Hawaii: a tropical paradise set on a volcanic ridge. The land that rises above the ocean's surface is nothing compared to what is standing beneath!**

## AN ISLAND CHAIN

**Hawaii is a U.S. state formed from eight islands and 124 islets. These islands are the peaks of a volcanic ridge formed deep beneath the ocean. Hawaii's position in the middle of the Pacific Plate means that the Hawaiian Islands are formed over a hotspot. The islands have a warm climate all year round with a regular rainfall. This creates the perfect climate for growing plants, and many are exported around the world.**

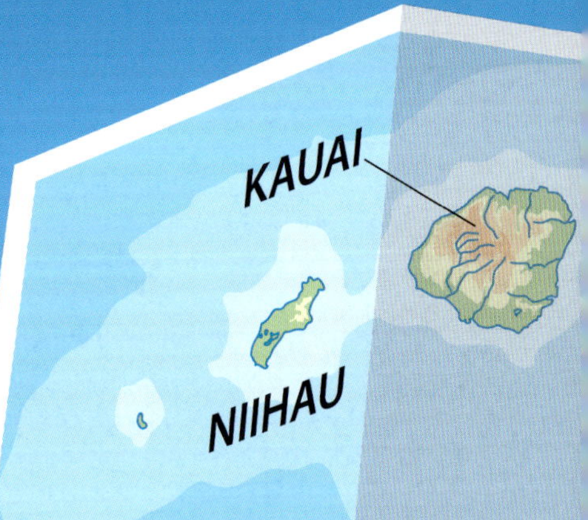

### 1 HAWAII STATE

The state of Hawaii has a mixed-ethnicity population made up of Polynesian, American, Asian, and European descendants. The capital city is Honolulu on Oahu island. There are no active volcanoes on Oahu, but there are extinct craters. Tourism, especially from those who come to surf, brings important income to the islands.

The 300,000-year-old Diamond Head Crater overlooks Hawaii's capital city, Honolulu.

### 2 THE BIG ISLAND

The largest island in the chain is called Hawaii, also known as the "Big Island." It is formed from five volcanoes: Mauna Loa, Kilauea, Mauna Kea, Hualalai, and Kohala. Mauna Loa and Kilauea are active today. Most eruptions are low level and are contained within the caldera at the summit – but occasionally they are bigger.

Mount Kilauea is the world's most active volcano. It's produced a river of lava that stretches 10 miles (16 km) to the sea.

## 3 THE TALLEST MOUNTAIN?

Mauna Kea rises 13,796 feet (4,205 m) above the ground – but it has another 19,685 feet (6,000 m) below sea level! Its total height is 33,497 feet (10,210 m), which is taller than Everest (see page 4). Perched on top of Mauna Kea is an observatory – the height and clear, dry conditions make the perfect stargazing spot!

# PEOPLE IN THE MOUNTAINS

**People have always been drawn to awesome mountain landscapes. Mountains are thrilling to climb and amazing for snow sports, but they can be challenging places to live in.**

## MOUNTAIN LIFE

Mountain areas provide many useful resources including minerals, timber, water, and scenery. The land can be fertile, which is good for growing crops, such as tea and coffee, and grazing animals. However, these areas also hold dangers, including avalanches, landslides, and earthquakes.

Fewer towns are built high up because of the difficulty of getting materials to them. Many mountain communities live in small villages and are well adapted to mountain life through centuries of living in this difficult environment.

People enjoy the Traditional Mask Dance Festival in the Spiti Valley in northern India, around 12,470 feet (3,800 m) above sea level.

## EXCITING ADVENTURES

Mountains are a huge draw for tourists who come to see spectacular scenery, amazing wildlife, thrilling snow sports, and more. They are a draw for climbers who seek to conquer new heights.

Visitors to these regions bring essential income to the people who live there, but they also bring problems. Building roads and places to stay damages natural ecosystems. Increased numbers of people in the area means more waste is created and more resources, such as power and water, are needed.

This popular ski resort in Italy has 74 miles (119 km) of slopes for visitors and 32 lifts to transport them up to the heights.

### MAP MASTERS

Maps are a great way to look at how land use changes. With the help of new technology, today's maps are detailed and accurate. They can show increased human activity and infrastructure, changing wildlife zones and landforms, river and coastal erosion, and changing weather patterns.

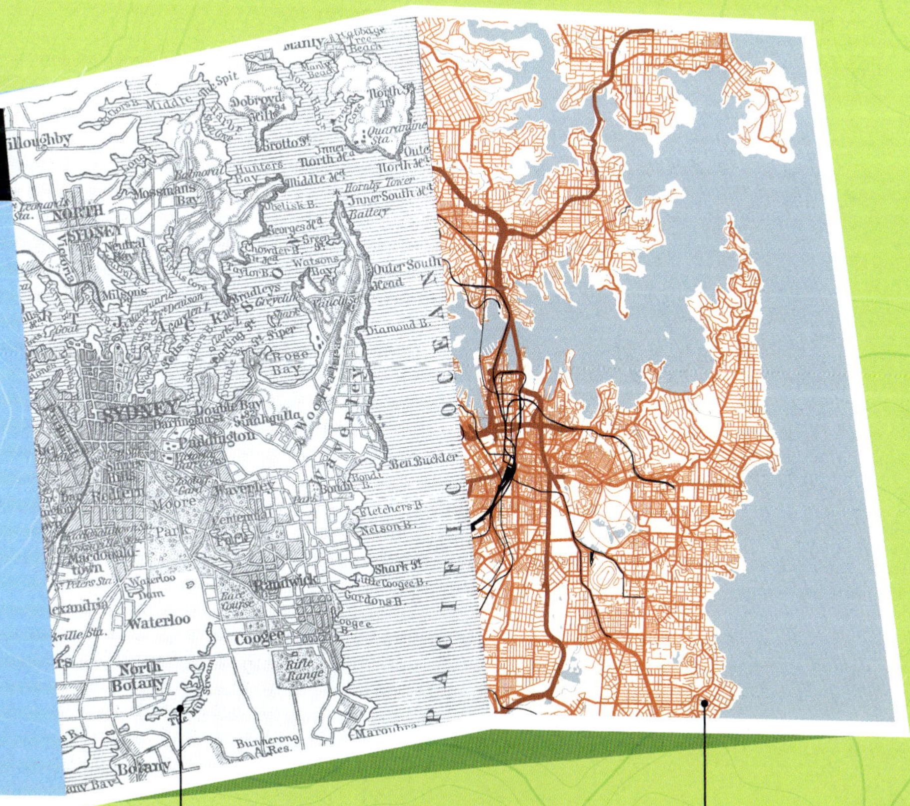


Sydney, Australia.
Left: around 1900. Right: today.

# MAPPING THE ALPS

The Alps are the biggest range of mountains in Europe. Parts of France, Monaco, Italy, Switzerland, Liechtenstein, Austria, Germany, and Slovenia are all in the Alps.

## CHANGING TIMES

**There is evidence of human life in the Alps as long as 60,000 years ago. Since that time, Celtic tribes, Romans, and Germanic tribes have all made their homes here. Later, roads, railways, and tunnels brought more industry to the mountains. This was once a mainly agricultural region, but today industries include mining, manufacturing, and – the biggest one – tourism.**

Ancient rock carvings can be found in Italy's Camonica Valley. They are thought to date from 8000 BCE.

### 1 RHÔNE RIVER

The source of the Rhône is a glacier high in the Alps. This great river flows through Lake Geneva and on through the fertile Rhône Valley to the Mediterranean Sea. The Rhône Valley is rich farming land with fruit and vegetable crops and vineyards.

## 2 INDUSTRY

The Alps once supported steel and paper industries, but today many resources have been exhausted and businesses have faced complications of getting supplies to this difficult inland region, as well as competition from other countries. Through the complications, specialized industry has thrived in Geneva. First established as a center of jewelry making, it then became famous for watchmaking and some important companies still have headquarters there today.

**FACT**

THERE ARE OVER 600 SKI RESORTS IN THE ALPS!

## 3 TOURISM

From 1945 onward, tourism in the Alps has boomed. Tourism jobs replaced many that were lost in the decline of industry and agriculture. The Alps have around 100 million visitors a year, but the region still faces challenges as the Alps' weather can change from year to year.

# GLOSSARY

**adapted** changed to fit a situation

**agriculture** farming, including growing crops and raising animals

**avalanche** a fall of snow or ice down a steep slope

**caldera** a volcanic crater that has collapsed in on itself

**climate** the weather patterns in a specific area

**debris** loose pieces of natural material or garbage that have been scattered about

**dormant** inactive

**ecosystem** all of the living things in an area and the way they affect each other

**ethnic group** a group of people who share the same cultural background

**extinct** (of a volcano) no longer active, with no record of eruption in recorded history

**fertile** describes soil that is good to grow plants in

**glacier** a river of ice that moves incredibly slowly

**granite** a hard type of rock formed from cooled magma or lava

**groundwater** water held underground in rock or soil

**ice cap** an area covered thickly with ice

**islet** a small island

**monsoon** wind that brings rains for a long period of time

**nickel** a silver-white metallic element

**photogrammetry** the use of photography in mapping to make measurements

**Polynesia** an area in the Pacific Ocean that includes the islands of Hawaii, the Marquesas Islands, Samoa, the Cook Islands, and French Polynesia

**summit** the highest point of a mountain

**terrain** the ground and its physical features

**vineyard** an area where grapevines are planted and the grapes used to make wine

# FURTHER INFORMATION

## Books

**Mountains (Fact Planet series)** by Izzi Howell (Franklin Watts, 2020)

**Mountains (World Feature Focus series)** by Rebecca Kahn (Franklin Watts, 2020)

**Mountains (GeoGraphics series)** by Izzi Howell (Franklin Watts, 2018)

## Websites

**www.dkfindout.com/uk/earth/mountains/what-is-mountain**

This DK Find Out! page has information about different types of mountains.

**www.bbc.co.uk/bitesize/topics/z849q6f/articles/z4g3qp3**

This site has information about how mountains form and tectonic plates.

**www.natgeokids.com/uk/discover/geography/physical-geography/structure-of-the-earth**

There is lots to discover on the National Geographic Kids website, including this page about the structure of the Earth.

# INDEX

animals 13, 19, 26

climbing 4, 13, 26, 27
contour lines 11

Earth's crust 6, 8, 9, 10, 14, 15, 16, 18, 22
earthquakes 6, 8, 18, 26
ecosystems 4, 13, 27, 29
erosion 11, 14, 15, 16, 19, 27
Everest 4, 13, 25

forests 5, 13, 14

industry 16, 28, 29

lakes 5, 16, 17, 19, 20, 21, 28

mountain ranges 5, 12
- Alps 4, 7, 28–29
- Andes 5, 8, 9
- Himalayas 12–13
- Sierra Nevada 16–17

national parks 15, 17, 21, 23

plants 4, 19, 24
plateaus 12, 14, 18–19, 20–21

rain forest 12, 13
rivers 5, 12, 19, 27
- American 16, 17
- Rhône 28
- Tongariro 20, 21

satellites 15, 23

tectonic plates 6, 7, 8, 9, 10, 12, 14, 18, 19, 20, 22, 24
tourism 23, 24, 27, 28, 29
trees 4, 17

valleys 7, 14, 16, 17, 20, 26, 28
volcanoes 6, 8, 9, 15, 18, 20, 21, 22, 23, 24

water 4, 11, 18, 19, 21, 26, 27
weather 4, 12, 16, 19, 27, 29
weathering *see* erosion